# Praise for Through My Eyes

"The author's transparency will help a lot of people confront and defeat their own obstacles. Young people will certainly benefit the most from this book. It should be a mandatory read for everyone who seeks to move to the next level in life."

*Westley T. Leonard,*
*Minister of Southside Church of Christ,*
*Orlando, FL*

"Through My Eyes was an excellent read that just kept getting better. It starts with an honest account of life experiences that one might consider drawbacks. Then provides valuable insights that reward the audience with the benefit of seeing how one can overcome adversity through God's grace. The honesty was refreshing and the details brought about dramatic tension that kept me in suspense. Brandy shows how faith and strong determination will reward you with perseverance. She shows the importance of sensitivity and compassion when someone undergoes a traumatic experience. The poems are all in truth and contain a good deal of wisdom."

*Courtney Simmons, Oakland, CA*

"A short read, it's filled with a lot of the author's personal experiences and challenges which can be applied to everyday life. I highly recommend this book, it's very inspiring."

*Ray Dennis, Jr., RR Donnelley,*
*Director of Global Business Services,*
*Chicago, IL*

"Seldom does such a short read tug at so many emotions at its onset. Brandy, I applaud your tenacity to continue and exceed where many others would have given up, as to your life story I can only reply more, more, and more!"

*Davie Laron, St. Louis, MO*

"This book of poetry is not only motivational but spiritually uplifting, also. Brandy captures her readers with such humility and transparency in the first few pages with chapter, *Behind the Mask*. Throughout this book I could feel the emotions Brandy displayed through her writings; whether it was love, happiness, sadness, angriness, or disbelief. As I continued to read, I was anxiously flipping the page to read more and I would often think to myself, "I can relate." I must admit that for anyone who reads this book will enjoy the uplifting spirit, empowering mindset, and her faith in Christ. Within the poetry, Brandy displays how pertinent it is to be considerate and subtle toward individuals who have experienced devastating trauma."

*Angela Williams, Police Officer, Shreveport, LA*

"I recommend this short read to any woman seeking a motivational addition to their coffee table or night stand reads. An amazing accomplishment and testament of a woman's work, this book is going to break your heart *and* warm it."

*Ann McQueen, Playwright, Riding Halley's Comet*

"*Through My Eyes* is truly an inspiration that crosses all social barriers. The collective information and style of presentation is motivating and unique. I sincerely feel the author accomplished her objective exemplifying hope in a sometimes hopeless world."

*Richard Perry, Retired Educator,*
*St. Louis Public Schools*

# THROUGH
*My Eyes*

**BRANDY GATES**

Southern Butterfly Entertainment

© 2017 by Brandy Gates. All rights reserved.

No part of this book may be reproduced in any written, electronic, recording, or photocopying form without written permission of the publisher. The exception would be in the case of brief quotations embodied in critical articles or reviews and pages where permission is specifically granted by the publisher.

Although every precaution has been taken to verify the accuracy of the information contained herein, the author and publisher assume no responsibility for any errors or omissions. Scripture quotations used in this book are from the Holy Bible, King James Version via TheHolyBibleApp.com. No liability is assumed for damages that may result from the use of information contained within.

Books may be purchased in quantity by contacting the publisher directly:
**SOUTHERN BUTTERFLY ENTERTAINMENT**
PO Box 603, St. Louis, MO 63188
SouthernButterfly.Org

ISBN: 978-0-9971232-0-3
Second Edition

Printed in the United States

# *Dedication*

As a compassionate person, it's difficult not to feel a way when life ends, especially in tragedy. For me, losing those I care about provides a re-birthing opportunity, unique process and perspective. With every death, is an opportunity to re-evaluate what's important, as well as the people and situations which are priorities. I dedicate this book to those who have touched me personally and those whose tragic circumstances deserve to be remembered and treasured.

Marsha Allen
Cheryl J. Mosely
Estella Roland
Siedah Mack
Shantaneika Collins
Danette L. Burse
Hurricane Katrina Victims
Virginia Tech Victims
Sandy Hook Elementary Victims

The Families of Sandra Bland, Michael Brown, Eric Garner,
Chris Kyle, Freddie Gray and Trayvon Martin.

To every family who has lost a loved one to senseless violence. I ask my Lord and Savior to bless each and every one.

# *Contents*

Behind The Mask.........................................................2
A Tale of Two Careers ................................................9
Explosion....................................................................14
Good Morning............................................................21
Laying In The Bed You Made...................................24
I Know .......................................................................28
At A Glance................................................................30
Looking For Love ......................................................33
Getting To Know Him...............................................36
When Will You Be Mine?..........................................40
Fly Girl........................................................................43
The Seasons................................................................46
Color Lines.................................................................49
Am I My Brother's Keeper? .....................................53
Friendship ..................................................................58
Time ............................................................................61
The Effects Of Death.................................................63
Good Night ................................................................65
A New Start................................................................68
10 Guidelines For A New Start ................................70
Acknowledgements ...................................................73
About The Author .....................................................76
About This Book........................................................78

*"I cannot think of any need in a childhood as strong as the need for a father's protection."*
~ Sigmund Freud

# *Behind The Mask*

— ৡ —

I need a healing for my soul and maybe you need one too. I wrote this book to help me heal from multiple traumatic incidents which took place in my life over the years. This is for me, for you, and for every person who wants to give up but knows they can't. There are a lot of broken people on the inside who try to mask their brokenness with make-up, hair weave, red bottom shoes, false eyelashes, cosmetic surgery to different parts of their bodies, designer purses, vehicles, designer watches and tennis shoes, clothes, electronics, and even use relationships/ lovers to mask the pain instead of facing it.

When I was eight years old I was sexually molested by my male cousin who was at least 18 at the time. He was grown enough to know better. I can remember him asking me to come into his room to see something. He told me I shouldn't be afraid or scared because I would like it. Of course, I complied. I don't remember if I thought that was strange or odd at the time, I just listened to my big cousin. I lay on the bed. He removed my underwear and then he stroked the head of his penis on the outside of my vagina and kind of played around with me to get me half way comfortable with being touched in that area. He tried to penetrate me but that didn't work – he could only get the tip inside because he was too big for my eight year old self. This lasted for just a little while. Then he told me to go take a bath.

I don't really remember how I felt afterward. I don't know if I felt like what I did was wrong or if what I did was bad. I just proceeded, after I took my bath, to do whatever my eight year old self was doing that day.

"It" happened about two or three more times before my mother found out. I was playing with one of my dolls and was acting out the things my cousin had done to me under the covers. When she saw this, she asked what I was doing. I replied, "Nothing mom." She said, "Yes, you were doing something. What were you doing?" Then she said I wasn't going to get in trouble for telling her what I was doing, so I explained that I was trying to make myself feel good with the doll. I was using the head of the doll as if it was my cousin's penis. My mother asked where I learned that from and I told her who taught me.

She explained to me that this wasn't appropriate to do, that he was wrong for what he did. In the end, she hugged me, she told me she loved me and that I shouldn't have had to experience such nasty things, especially with someone in my family. She explained that sex was for adults and it wasn't something I should be worried about as a kid. After that day I was never permitted to go back to my biological paternal grandmother's home.

I didn't go to counseling, nor were charges pressed against my cousin.

As I type this, I'm thankful that I didn't turn out to be a promiscuous teenager, that I didn't become a teenage mom, and that I became protective of my body. I realize I have a tough outer shell now – likely because I never want anyone to see me as weak or dare think they can take advantage of me.

As an adult, no one ever wants to admit they've been molested by someone in their family even though they know it wasn't their fault because they feel ashamed, worried about how others will look at them, that people will alienate them as if they are taboo, and they don't want to feel pitied either.

I didn't have my biological father present to protect me from incidents like this. He was an absentee father, and being violated by my cousin only contributed to the feelings I already had of abandonment, rejection, and feeling like I was a mistake.

As a girl, you expect your father to protect you from bad people in the world, to rectify situations – especially when someone violates you, and when that doesn't happen, you carry a burden, thinking,

*Why did this happen to me?* You learn that bad things happen to good people and through love, faith and prayer, you can eventually come to terms with things, whether you understand them at that time or not. You have to decide if you want to become better or just remain bitter.

Through my spiritual journey and finding God, I never thought this would come back to haunt me in my adult life because when you learn about God, His love, and His forgiveness, you learn that by the blood of Christ you are cleansed and made whole. Although you may not feel that way on the inside because you still may have the memory or the scars of the damage which was done. But you are given hope for a fresh start, a do-over, and are promised you can live a life of joy, peace, and happiness even through the emotions which at times erupt as you look back on your life and experiences.

I'm reliving the experience in this moment, feeling the pain, the guilt, the dirtiness of what happened as I accept my truth. It hurts but I press through so that I will not let my fears keep me from meaningful, loving relationships. I pray and hope God will send my mate the one who will love me the right way – treating me with appreciation, support, loyalty and love - protecting me the way I need to be protected. One who won't abandon me when things become difficult.

I suppose it hasn't happened yet because I wasn't ready to receive him...this is why I was honest and open about the need for, desire to and acceptance of healing for me and for any of you who have been violated, fearful or felt unprotected.

I don't know why God chose me to walk the journey I was given. However, this experience has taught me how to be very detailed in the way I communicate with others, very deliberate in expressing my feelings, very sincere in expressing my love and affection for family and friends, and it has also taught me not to take people for granted and not to make assumptions about other people's lives.

What doesn't kill you will make you stronger. Every storm will test your character, courage and perseverance. Embracing your truth gives you a powerful voice, if you decide to listen to God and follow His direction because everything in your life is ordered by divine design and there is always a blessing in your lesson.

Looking for love, acceptance, intimacy, affection and someone who cares about you temporarily, is not a substitute for someone who will love you, care about you and treat you well for the marathon. Being "ready for the race" takes conditioning, training, discipline, determination and confidence. Self-esteem is a key factor in overcoming the past. Don't allow fear of rejection, abandonment or feeling like others won't accept you because of your past stop you from winning your race.

Through God's love, understanding your flaws, and embracing your truth, you can learn to forgive yourself, and not allow your circumstances, situations, or things which are temporary hold you back, or keep you from walking in your purpose.

*"Your life can be anything you desire it to be as long as you believe it, create a plan with some strategy, and work it, you can achieve it. I pray that everyone who reads my poetry will gain some knowledge, wisdom, and insight about themselves, and even a new outlook on life."*
~ Brandy Gates

# A Tale of Two Careers

I am fortunate enough to have two careers, one in law enforcement and the other as a reservist in the military. Between 2009 and 2011 I graduated from the police academy, basic training in the military, Builder A school through the Navy and began my first assignment on the St. Louis Metropolitan Police Department. It sounds good now but it was a long journey to get here.

Growing up on the streets of Oakland, California, I saw a lot of police brutality on the news and in real life. During my formative years the Rodney King beating and subsequent verdict was just one of the many incidents which was not only memorable but also devastating to people around me. I took it personally. I wanted to know why justice did not prevail. I was incensed by the blatant racism & prejudice against blacks in America – that which was happening routinely and that which was actually captured on national television.

As a young black girl in America, I was drawn to the profession of Law Enforcement because of all the disparities and unfair practices that I saw with my own eyes. I wanted to be able to arrest individuals who were pedophiles, violent criminals, thieves and drug dealers who make our communities unsafe, crippled, abandoned and run down. I wanted justice and was willing to put my life on the line to get it, but not immediately. I needed to live a little first, and I thought going to college would keep me out of poverty. I learned that wasn't necessarily true.

When I graduated high school in 1996, I attended Louisiana Tech University in Ruston, Louisiana. I graduated in four years and started working as a manager at a large retail chain in Shreveport, Louisiana. After four years I needed a change of pace and environment so I relocated to St. Louis, Missouri. Living in St. Louis has been a mixed bag.

I worked for a very well known rental car company for two years. I loved the work and was excelling in every area. Then one day I was moved to a location in Kirkwood, Missouri, a suburb of St. Louis, where I was treated horribly by the branch manager and many of the customers. I was continually disrespected, and made to feel intimated by fear and humiliated by words, actions and unsatisfactory performance evaluations. It was shocking and obvious that the manager did not like nor appreciate me for who I am – a goal-oriented, hard working, educated black woman who was excelling within the company.

One day he changed the rules for my non-Black female counterpart and chastised me for following company protocol. He invited me to leave for the day – something I did – permanently. The frustration had been building for quite some time. I felt sending me to that location had sabotaged my career. I wish I had not made the emotional decision to leave based on his treatment of me, but I did. Customer and peer views of race played such a huge factor. That was also the first and last time I quit a job without having another lined up. Because of that decision, I ended up being unemployed for about a year. I was extremely close to going back to the life I once knew as a young person growing up in the projects though I had a degree, job experience and strong work ethic.

When I became unemployed I felt very lost – in identity and in purpose. It was difficult for me to grasp why I couldn't get a job with my background, skill set and qualifications. It was one of the lowest points of my life. I could see why people might turn to drugs or consider suicide as a viable option, how women choose prostitution as an option; and I also learned who my real friends were, along with the true meaning of friendship. During that year my confidence and self-esteem were at an all-time low. I didn't believe I could recover from that situation. I was alone in St. Louis without friends or family. For the first time in my life I thought I would get evicted. Many times I didn't know how I would pay my full rent, even with unemployment, and it terrified me. It made me want to give up because it was easier to do that than to continue to fight and have hope that there was something better for me and that there was really a purpose for my life.

My spiritual mom was very supportive. She prayed with me, encouraged me, and kept telling me not to give up. It helped so much because she was in the same city. She helped me grow in the Lord, and in my faith – as I learned to truly trust God.

During my time of unemployment I applied for the St. Louis Metropolitan Police Department and also joined the military. I needed to save my own life and possibly the lives of others.

Being a police officer has allowed me to fight for justice, be fair in the quality of my investigations and arrests, influence fellow officers, and to make a difference for those in the communities I serve. It's fulfilling, it's exciting and it's adventurous. I love the daily challenges, the things I learn and the new experiences because nothing is routine in police work. Having a good rapport with those in the community is how I vowed to protect and serve which is also essential, and I take pride in helping people feel comfortable to talk to me, and share any information that may help me make good arrests on those who make neighborhoods unsafe.

I joined the military because it was a guaranteed option to permanently remove me from the negative, drug infested, gang saturated and impoverished community in which I grew up, which has become the norm for most Black Americans who have grown up in the projects like I did. Through enlisting in the United States Navy, I have been able to get a free education, have great benefits, become an expert in carpentry and literally seen the world. It may sound like a commercial but, it's true for me and I appreciate the experience, though it hasn't always been easy. The other side of war, in the trenches is gritty, dirty, scary, stressful and mentally exhausting. As a woman serving my experiences taught me how to have thick skin, how to stand up for myself, how to believe in my abilities, how to conquer my fears and how to overcome obvious and subtle obstacles which could have killed me. I've learned to be assertive and to stand up for myself when others couldn't relate or simply didn't want to.

# Explosion

I had bottled in hurt and pain from being on deployment. It gave me plenty of time to think about home, coupled with feelings of isolation, these thoughts made me come to grips about being angry. I was angry about events in my life and also about my dad not being there. Each confrontation with my squad leader brought more agitation. He did not relate to me nor did we have decent communication. We were confined to a small space on the base. I tried working out to relieve stress but that could only go so far. There wasn't anything to distract me from thinking about my problems. Every day we focused on staying alive, and on keeping our people alive and safe. Other than that, dealing with what was on the inside was what I was up to. The people around me would make plans to socialize during downtime but I was never included or invited to participate. I feel like I had a lot in common with some of them but they didn't feel the same, as evidenced by their actions.

On September 16, 2014, at North Kabul Compound (NKC), Kabul Afghanistan the base was hit with a Vehicle Borne Incendiary Explosive Device (VBIED) attack. Just prior to the explosion I was standing front door watch at 8am praying to God about how thankful I was just to see another day. Shortly after I finished praying, I heard the biggest "BOOM" of my life. I heard the VBIED explosion go off within 50 meters of where I was standing watch. It was so strong that the vibration shook the entire compound which felt like a 6.0 Earthquake. I saw a red/orange bursts, then a huge black/grey funnel cloud. The force of the explosion pushed me into the wall I was guarding, causing me to lose consciousness.

When I regained consciousness I saw the funnel cloud of smoke approaching me in a rapid manner, I took cover to avoid inhaling the fumes and debris from the explosion. I listened first to see if there was going to be a second explosion and after I didn't hear anything I stepped to the side opening to make sure the wall wasn't breached. Then I listened for gun fire – all I heard was dead silence. I remained at my post continuing to stand front door watch as individuals were given the clear to leave the smaller bunkers and enter the building I was guarding. At some point I remember thanking God again for saving me and also praying for the six ISAF (International Security Assistance Force) soldiers who were killed.

My body and mind were definitely in shock however there was no time to deal with my body or mind. I had a job to do. I had been trained to respond, react, to communicate, to stop the threat or deal with the threat, and to be accountable to those in command. I did all that. My training got me through the initial stages of the attack on NKC.

Immediately after I verified identities and got our personnel into the building safely, I began to cry uncontrollably as my emotions and adrenaline were very high. One of the Army Medical Commanders noticed it and relieved me of my watch duty. He sent me to the medical triage area to get evaluated. I was put under a 48 hour lockdown observation to monitor all of my behavior and motor functioning skills to access if there was any damage. I went through a series of tests and was diagnosed as having Traumatic Brain Injury (TBI). I began having severe migraine headaches, restless nights of sleep, dizziness, and chest pains daily. I was prescribed Tylenol 500mg for my migraine headaches and Benadryl to help me sleep. After several days had passed, I still was not able to process what happened, though I tried. I am very thankful that the blast didn't kill me and that the explosion didn't breach the t-walls (big cement block walls designed to help protect the base in case of explosions). I was very confused and my emotions were all over the place. I didn't know how I was supposed to feel or act, and I didn't really know who I was or who I was supposed to be after experiencing such a traumatizing event. I felt like a stigma, as if everyone was looking at me crazy, and I felt alone.

My Squad Leader and Fire Team Leaders showed no support emotionally or physically after the experience. My days became more depressing, and dreadful. I became angry towards my co-workers as well because no one who I worked directly with or for showed compassion, understanding or sensitivity to my unstable condition. I had six weeks between the time of the explosion and being able to return home. Thankfully, my Senior Chief, Safety Chief and Lieutenant were supportive and stable figures who helped me get through that tough time and finish out my deployment.

Upon my return to the States, I received treatment in Norfolk, Virginia to get healthy and whole before returning home to my family. My treatment included seeing a psychologist, occupational therapist, behavioral therapist, a neurologist and I attended group therapy for a week. I still have flashbacks from time to time and I often reflect back over my life whenever I face something challenging in order to remember how far God has brought me. Being alive reminds me that I'm here for a purpose and He's not done with me yet.

Going through the explosion made me look at myself and life a lot differently. It made me want to heal and get better – from the new pain and from the past pain. I had to let go of what wasn't important and work through what was.

Many people, though not necessarily physically injured, don't know how to deal with the mental aspects of going through IED explosions and the aftermath. The military mindset about breaking down and crying is that those actions make us appear weak. We've learned to suppress instead of talking about what happened and recovering from the experience.

It's pretty sad because you can't just pick your life up from where you left off and act like the horror didn't happen but unfortunately, too many do. That's why people get divorced and depressed – because showing emotions is not acceptable. Too many people try to numb the pain through alcohol and other substances. I understand it, but it will never go away unless you deal with your truth.

Families and spouses need to understand the importance of getting support for the affected loved one – even when they say nothing's wrong, especially when they say nothing's wrong. Don't leave it there and don't just run away. It's difficult. Our training teaches us what to do however, life afterward, untreated, will allow what didn't kill us to implode inside of us as time moves on.

When you go through traumatic experiences in a combat zone you become somebody new and you have to find out who this new person is. What defines you will change. Your life will have a new meaning. It's up to you to keep searching, get help, and keep standing.

I've shared a bit about my life because after all, the book is titled, "Through My Eyes." It's been a bit uncomfortable, difficult and emotional sharing my experiences however; I needed to give you a bit of my perspective if I expect my poetry to touch your heart and my 10 Guidelines for a Fresh Start to be used by you. I feel the strength of my faith has gotten me through and I am honored to share a bit with you.

*"I'm fulfilled in what I do...I never thought that a lot of money or fine clothes---the finer things of life---would make you happy. My concept of happiness is to be filled in a spiritual sense."*

~ Coretta Scott King

# *Good Morning*

Dear Heavenly Father,
Thank you for waking me up this morning
In my right mind with all my health and strength.
Thank you for allowing me to see just one more day.
As I start my day, please protect me from the fiery darts of Satan,
Grant me traveling grace to make it to and from my destinations,
And allow me to make it back home safely.
Grant me the wisdom, knowledge and discernment I need to make good
Decisions throughout my day to day activities.
Please forgive me of my sins and transgressions daily,
So that I may grow stronger in spirit and in truth
I pray that you watch over all of my family, friends, co-workers and
All those who are dear to me.
Protect them from harm, evil, and temptation.
I pray for the sick and the shut in,
That their health be restored.

That your grace will see them through another day.
I pray for ministers, the leadership of their congregations that
They'll continue to guide them in spirit, wisdom, and understanding,
That they may stay strong, as fighting soldiers, on the battlefield for you.
Thank you for the many blessings you have bestowed on my life
And for those yet to come.
I pray that I will continue to let my light shine
Ever so brightly that it may not be hidden,
No matter where I may go.
I pray for humility so that you can use me as you see fit
To be effective in your kingdom,
Lord I ask all these blessings in your Son
Jesus' name I pray,
Amen.

*"Character is like a tree, and reputation like its shadow. The shadow is what we think of it; the tree is the real thing."*

~ Abraham Lincoln

# Laying In The Bed You Made

Ladies,
Where do your priorities lie?
Why will many of us become
A baby mama before becoming a wife?
Why will you conveniently put yourself
In the position to experience pain and strife
Because of decisions you've made in life?

I'm not trying to call anyone out
But let's be honest, this is something
which needs to be talked about.
It's time to break this cycle, break the chains,
By learning from our mistakes,
Teaching our children how to be better,
No matter what it takes;
Why not instill in our children from birth,
The importance of getting an education, discipline and wisdom
To make it easier in life?
God says, "The fear of the Lord is the beginning of knowledge,
But fools despise wisdom and instruction."

How many times are you going to lie down on
your back to
Get what you think you want?
How long will it take you to tap into the wisdom
that
God makes available to you?
When you start to use your mind, only then
Will you get up off your behind.
Why is it that you have money to spend
To obtain the look of a Hollywood Star,
But when you look in the mirror
You don't even know who you are?
You faithfully spend money going out to the club,
but
Won't spend $20 dollars on a book that will teach
you about love?
Meanwhile you can't decipher between what's fake
and what's real
Because all you're looking for is a cheap thrill.

How much time do you spend elevating your
mind, verses
Giving your body up to drunkenness
And being filled in excess with wine?
Reading is fundamental, this I know,
If you never plant seeds in life, how can you grow?
Grow to reap a gigantic harvest of overflow,
Filled with all kinds of fruit.
Stretch your wings and fly
Get rid of all the gossip, deceit, negativity and lies.
Be what God destined you to be by
Living in reality, and reality is

If you don't put on a glove
When it's time to make love
You're dumb and soon to be dead
Because with all the cases of AIDS reported
There is NOTHING LEFT TO BE SAID.

The true reason for having sex is to be fruitful and multiply
And every time you're having sex you
Become one with him, and that's no lie.
Sisters, close your legs and stop selling yourself short
So you won't have to make a decision of whether
Or not to abort and cover up a bad decision you've made.
It's time to be more responsible by lying in the bed you made.

*"Without education, you are not going anywhere in the world!"*

~ Malcolm X

# I Know

I know I was born only to die
I know I will laugh more than I will cry
I know I will get married and have some kids
I know that I have a gorgeous smile
With conversation that can last awhile
I know troubles will only last for a short time
I know when I get on this mic, I speak my mind
While allowing my light to shine
I know I have a lot of love to give
But how long will I be blessed to live
I know I have soft lips
And proportionate hips
I know some people think I am naïve
But it's better to give than to receive
I know as long as I have a mouthpiece
I will use it and not abuse it
I know I am somebody's daughter, somebody's child
I know someone wants to love me and make me smile
I know my time here on earth is only for a little while
I know, I know, I know.

*"Excellence is not a skill. It is an attitude."*
~ Ralph Marston

# At A Glance

How do you find the words
To say what's on your mind?
Do you tell that brotha or sista
You find him or her fine?

It is something about the person
Who puts a smile on your face
It makes you wonder,
Should you try to get with that person
Or should you stay in your place
And smile as you have always done.

It is amazing how one person makes another blush
It could be the soft touch of a hand,
The sweet smells of perfume or cologne,
Or it could be the glow that you see in each other's eyes.
You wonder is this a line you want to cross or not…
Your choices are, we can be friends until the end
Or you can try to capture his or her heart.

In the end, you don't want to wonder
What could have been if I would have tried
Because you usually won't have any regrets
And most importantly you put forth the effort
Which is the best thing you can do.

Always remember have faith in yourself and
In all that you do while keeping the Lord first
And just take it one day at a time.

*"Everybody likes a compliment."*
~ Abraham Lincoln

# *Looking For Love*

As you take a long walk, you look around outside
Admiring the clouds in the sky, inhaling the cool breeze and fresh air
Slowly, gently and delicately
You're in awe with the amazing view
And then you notice someone looking at you.

Your eyes meet with an intense stare
Then softly run your fingers through your hair
He graces your eyes with his amazing smile
He keeps hypnotizing with his gaze
As you listen to the sound of crashing waves
Your desire to find that special someone
Is what you dreamed of many days.

As he begins to walk towards you
You suddenly feel a strong pull of energy
From his body to yours
From your soul to his
As you leave footprints in the sand,

He comes over and takes your hand
And begins to walk with you
You are both headed towards your future, your destiny.

*"There can be no deep disappointment where there is not deep love."*
> ~ Martin Luther King, Jr.

# Getting To Know Him

I wanna know your name
And who you are
From the food you eat
Down to the way you sleep
I wanna know
How do you treat women?
Do you know our value?
Do you know our worth?
How well connected are you
With Mother Nature's earth?
I know your job is to
Make people laugh, but
What I am wondering is
Who is the man behind the mask?

I know your date of birth
As well as your zodiac sign
You say you're looking forward
To meeting me in due time
What is it about me that impresses you

I am not quite sure
I love your southern accent
And can't wait to hear more
That is more conversation
Of mental stimulation
That elevates me deeply
I can tell you that
I'm not looking for a man
To complete me
Just a man that wants to be with me, and only me.
I am already complete.

I need a man that will
Treat me the way
He wants to be treated
I need a man that doesn't give up
Or is easily defeated
I hope you are not trying to run game
Because if you are that is pretty lame
If you're looking for someone that is genuine and real
Then I am the one and I even have
A little bit of sex appeal
I need a man that can help me grow to new heights,
Tell me, are you trying to make this same flight
While on this journey called life?
I need a man that will lift me up and not tear me down
A man that can make me turn a frown into a smile

A man that cherishes being in my presence
If only for a little while
From what I know so far, you're kind of wonderful
That is what you are
Oh, and one last thing
Do you feel, you have what it takes
To be down on my team?

*"If any man will come after me, let him deny himself, and take up his cross daily and follow me."*
~ Luke 9:23

# *When Will You Be Mine?*

It's a pretty day let's go outside
Unless you have something else in mind then
I'm all for it because as long as I'm with you I will enjoy it.
What is it about you that drives me crazy, insane
It's because you talk to me with your eyes
Which let's me know what's on your mind,
Oh baby, love is something you deserve
But something you have to earn
My love is honest and true
Tell me, what you want me to do?
I can prove it to you
That I am commitment worthy
But that's only if you're ready to step out
And make the journey.
My love is everything you need only if you choose it,
But if you don't take out the time to pursue it
You will lose it, lose out on the best opportunity for love
Next to, the love from God above.
I am so amazing in many ways that

I can make an old man wish for younger days
I want a man that is strong, kind, intelligent
And oh so fine.

You see, I liked him so much it turned into love,
And love is living life through your ups and downs
Past the pain and strife
Now from love back to life.
He's like everything I dreamed of
And better than the preview
He's fine like the earth, the sea, and the sky
I want to give him the keys to my heart and that's
no lie
Us together is like the stars in the sky
There would be no limit as to how high we can fly
He's like the food I eat, and I need food to survive
You need to remember how to make believe
Because true love captures
Your heart, soul and mind
Love will make you give a person your last dime
While capturing the essence of time
I only have one question,
When will you be mine?

*"Who can find a virtuous woman? For her price is far above rubies."*

~ Proverbs 31:10

# Fly Girl

Hey fly girl what's your name?
Those jeans look so good on you
I would put them in the hall of fame.
You are a shining star
The apple of my eye
I have to admit girl your style is really fly.

What do I need to do, to get next to you?
Can I walk you home from school or
Carry your books to class?
If that doesn't work, then I'll buy you some flowers
Or tell you some jokes to make you laugh.
You have that "It" factor
I wonder what could it be
Is it your delightful conversation or
Those precious dimples I see?
Is it the sway in your hips or
Those sweet, soft, sensual lips?
Whatever it is, I have to see you
At least once a day just to get my fix
If I could, I would be a fly on the wall
So when that other brother messes up

I can catch you when you fall and
Protect you like a queen
From all the playas, pimps and wanna be's
Well you know what I mean.
I just wanna be down on your team
I can't wait to hold your hand
And give you a big hug
While I stare deeply into your dark brown eyes
Knowing that I will be your guy
Gorgeous you're the only one
That I want in the whole world
Because you are the finest, my fly girl.

*"We may encounter many defeats but we must not be defeated."*

~ Maya Angelou

# The Seasons

There are four seasons in all
You have winter,
You have spring,
You have summer
And last the fall.
Which season is the best for you?
Is it the spring, which is captivating with flowers, trees, and
A cool spring breeze.
In the spring, you get a lot of rain
Which reminds you of tears that help to ease your pain.

Moving on to those beautiful and hot summer days
Where sunshine fills the sky with its illuminating rays
Summer is a great time to go outdoors
Enjoy fishing, camping, water skiing and so much more
Then there is the grace of fall.
When the leaves begin to fade, changing colors

And then they must fall.
The beauty of it all is you fall only to rise again
And then your mind becomes clear,
Clear as the autumn's night
Where mellow thoughts remain
Before you're asleep snug and tight.
Last the winter is very pretty, yet so cold.
Many times it is a duplicate of how people can be
Because I know like you know
That misery loves company.
As you watch the soft and gentle snow falling
down
Sometimes you feel that you can melt with it
Just as it falls to the ground.

Everyone goes through seasons according to his or
her life,
And that is God's way of letting you know that
everything will be alright.

*"To everything there is a season, and a time to every purpose under the heaven a time to be born, and a time to die; a time to plant and a time to pluck up that which is planted. A time to kill, a time to heal, a time to break down, and a time to build up. A time to weep, and a time to laugh, a time to mourn, and a time to dance."*

~ Ecclesiastes 3:1-8

# *Color Lines*

As you look at my face,
Why can't you see past my race?
Why do I have to be a black woman
Or a black girl
How you view me is a concern
I am not bitch nor am I a hoe
I am educated, sophisticated, compassionate, and kind
How can we break down these color lines?

When I talk, why do you expect to hear slang
And when I talk with common sense
It drives you insane
Too bad I don't fit the stereotype
That you had portrayed in your mind
I am much more than my breasts, hips, and behind
How can we break down these color lines?
Why is it that you feel the only way to relate to us,
Is by what you see on videos or hear through music
When you walk past a black man
You clutch your purse as if he's going to steal it

Why do you continue to look at us
As an inferior race?
Or as people you feel the need to put in their place
How can we break down these color lines?

Why is everything associated with negativity
blamed on our race
But you have always wanted to sleep with us
Just so you can have a taste
Of what's soft, sensual, and sweet
I see you can't get enough of this dark meat
How can we break down these color lines?

Then you turn around and call us
Lazy, ignorant, and stupid
We cleaned your house while nursing, and raising
your children
We plowed your fields, cooked all of your meals
Only for you to get rich
Because you wouldn't pay us with dollar bills
How can we break down these color lines?

These are the only color lines you want to see
Because of your own insecurities you try to belittle
me
Keeping me focused on the wrong thing
Out of site out of mind
Is what I've been told
Because at the end of the rainbow
There is pot of gold.

We will break down these color lines with
Unity, love, knowledge, unselfishness,
perseverance
And persistence equates power
What are you willing to do to make a change,
So that we can all view these color lines the same?

*"I look to a day when people will not be judged by color of their skin, but by the content of their character."*
~ Martin Luther King, Jr.

# *Am I My Brother's Keeper?*

My brothers, my dear sweet brothers
What is your problem?
Why must you wear your pants
Hanging off of your butt?
Why do you encourage women
To dress like sluts just
To fulfill the lusts in your eyes
Instead of telling that sister
Your skirt is too short darling
It shouldn't be above your thighs
How many times are you gonna
Keep pushing that rock
From door to door and
On every other block
Just to get that quick paper
Only to one day get busted
By an undercover cop
It's amazing to me you'll stand
Out on the corner come rain, come shine
But say you won't work a 9-5
Because it's a waste of your time
Sounds to me like you need some

More discipline and discipleship in your life
Because if you don't change your ways
You're headed down the road of pain and strife
Am I my brothers' keeper?

It's amazing to me that you
Will be a keeper of lies, mistrust, and deceit
but you won't take a stand
To clean up your street, your neighborhood, or your home
And now you have allowed
your territory to become the danger zone
For drugs, alcohol, murder and high school dropouts
All because you refuse to speak out
And stand firm for what's right
But then you wonder why
Your child gets smoked in a gun fight
Now you're furious, enraged and
Want to see justice done
And you will now protect yourself by getting a gun
Saying I wish a man would come and try to rob my house
Because if he does
I am going to blow his brains out.
You are only perpetuating the cycle with this attitude
And becoming a part of the problem
Instead a part of the solution
Now it's time for the evolution
Am I my brother's keeper?

Brothers it is time that you become mentors,
A big brother to a child helping to develop
His character, mind and smile
Teaching him that crime doesn't pay
And if you want to earn money here is another way.
Showing him how to wash dishes,
do laundry, how to cook,
And take care of the lawn, that way
He won't be a stranger to hard and honest work
While teaching him how to be a man
You will even show him how to be entrepreneur
Verses him sitting back, up on his behind
And he will understand the importance,
The value of earning and spending his own dime
Instead of robbing, stealing and taking what's not his
While I'm on this road let me drop this by
Who told you it was healthy for you to get high on weed.
How about getting high on knowledge that comes from books
And books come free at the library
Oh I forgot, the thought of you obtaining knowledge
Must make you paranoid
Teach him how to balance a checkbook,
so he will only spend money he has
Instead of showing him, if you don't have the cash,
Then the plastic will have to be my pass.
My pass to buy me what I want
Drop that, buy now — pay later mentality and focus

*Brandy Gates*

on reality
That if this is your spending habits
You will be swimming in debt as you begin to sink really fast
Am I my brother's keeper?
Stop dropping your seeds in every town
All over the world.
If you owe it, just pay it
If you don't want to pay child support
Find yourself a wife first,
He that finds a wife finds a GREAT thing
Women weren't meant to be baby making machines
To any Tom, Dick, or Harry
As you really look at this, it's very scary.
Finally my brothers, hold fast to which is good
Don't stay a victim mentally of what's in the hood.
Rise up and take more responsibility
Become educated, dedicated, and driven achievers
Be determined not to let anyone turn you around
From being better Father's, Brothers, Friends, Christians and Lovers
Because God is the keeper of your life
When will you become God's keeper
By making him, your Wife?

*"The ultimate measure of a man is not where he stands in moments of comfort and convenience, but where he stands at times of challenge and controversy."*
~ Martin Luther King, Jr.

# *Friendship*

Life is a garden, good friends are the flowers,
And times spent together
Are life's happiest hours….

Friendship, like flowers blooms ever more fair
When carefully tended by dear friends who care.
I just want you to know that
The times we spend together are very special to me.
As time goes by, I value our friendship ever more.

Friendship is something that needs nurturing,
Cultivation and love.
Sometimes a friend needs you to listen
Sometimes a friend needs you to be objective
Sometimes a friend needs your advice
But most importantly,
A friend should always tell you what is right.

Do I become your enemy instead of your friend
When I tell you the truth?
A friend doesn't tell you what you want to hear,

But will give you wisdom and knowledge,
So that your thoughts become clear.
A friend will give you constructive criticism
And cut you where it hurts the most
Because when you hear the truth
It's sharper than a two-edged sword.

Friends are far, few and in between
If you have been blessed to have friends in your life
Make sure you tell them
Just how much they mean to you.

Send them their flowers
While they can still smell them
Because it makes the difference
In keeping a friend, or losing a friend.
Remember no one cares how much you know,
Until they know how much you care.

*"Love is the only force capable of transforming an enemy into a friend."*

~ Martin Luther King, Jr.

# *Time*

Time is cyclical
Time is slow
Time is very precious
Nevertheless, some may not know
Time is something you have very little of
The Lord has blessed you with so much from above
So, set aside some time to give him thanks.

In this lifetime,
Do not take things for granted
For nothing is promised, so
Live only for today, and not for tomorrow.

There is a time to sleep and
There is a time to eat
There is a time to work and
There is a time to play
However, do not think
These things are guaranteed every day.
Live each day as if it's your last
Do not live for the future
And do not live in the past
Live for this day, this minute, this second.

*"Let go of your attachment to being right, and suddenly your mind is more open. You're able to benefit from the unique viewpoints of others, without being crippled by your own judgment."*

~ Ralph Marston

# *The Effects Of Death*

How does death effect you?
Does death make you sad, angry, happy or numb?
Have you ever lost someone that you truly loved
Or that had an influential impact on your life?
If you have, then you understand how I feel.
I remember her smile, I remember her laugh,
I remember the last hug that she gave to me.
I remember our talks, I remember our walks
And last I remember our cries
And sometimes you ask the question,
Why God, why? The only answer is it was her time to go.

For you don't know the day,
The hour, nor when your time will come.
For your time here on earth
Is only temporary, a short little while
So don't believe you're going to live to grow old
Because the shooting at Virginia Tech
Will be the greatest story ever told.
You can never prepare for the death
And it will always hurt
So maximize the time you have
While living on this earth.

*"Trust in the lord with all thy heart; and lean not unto thy own understanding. In all thy ways acknowledge him, and he shall direct thy paths. Be not wise in thy own eyes; fear the Lord, and depart from evil."*
~ Proverbs 3:5-7

# *Good Night*

Dear Heavenly Father,
Thank you for watching over me throughout my day
And allowing me to make it back home safe and sound
I pray Lord that you put my mind as ease
As I prepare to go to sleep
That I will rest peacefully
And get the best quality sleep possible.
Thank you Lord for watching over
All of my family and friends today
Please forgive me of my sins and transgressions daily
So that I may grow stronger in spirit and in truth
It is only because of your grace
That I was able to make it through another day
Continue to protect me from all harm and danger.
Thank you for the many blessings that
You have bestowed on my life
Thank you for my trials, and my storms
Because without them I couldn't learn
Life's lessons or increase my faith in your word.

Please continue to keep me on the path of righteousness
As I continue to learn the purpose you have for my life
I pray for knowledge, wisdom, discernment and understanding
And I thank you in advance for my day tomorrow.
I ask all these things and blessings in your son Jesus Christ name I pray,
Amen.

*"Forgiveness is not an occasional act: it is an attitude."*
~ Martin Luther King, Jr.

# *A New Start*

Forgiving yourself and others for shortcomings and mistakes is crucial to being joyful, healthy and whole. Mistakes are teachable moments which require making corrections to move forward. It's not where you stop and stay, it's what you create in a new day. When you're unwilling to forgive others, you give them power over your emotional well-being. You're unable to move forward and you hinder your own progress because you are in your own way. When you begin to understand God's grace and how He forgives you for what you have done, and loves you in spite of your mistakes, only then will you begin to look at others and their flaws compassionately. It's time to release any pain which may be holding you back. Get out of your own way!

**Each New Day Can Be A Fresh Start**

Death of a loved one, disease, family struggles and failure can cripple even the strongest person. These are the times it's important to reach beyond the deep despair and choose to rise above the storms, tribulations and circumstances, using those things as your motivation, drive and passion to walk in your purpose. I've learned what it's like to be rejected. When I lost my job I went through serious depression because I didn't have income and found myself alone…things were so difficult… I wanted to numb the pain…God had to take me down to nothing for me to discover I was something. I was less than 50 feet away from being killed in an explosion – the physical one and the aftermath of dealing with it… traumatized; I found it difficult to move forward each day. What's been holding you back? Emotional struggle? Doubt? I wanted to quit many times. I didn't and you can't either. Finding a fresh start in each new day is the way…

Everything you do starts with your mindset. We all have routines, and things we do consciously and subconsciously based on the past and our experiences.

A big part of a fresh start has to do with changing how and what you think and then changing what and how you do things to get new results.

Removing negative thoughts, replacing them with positive affirmations, confidence and action is the beginning of a fresh start. In closing, I've shared my 10 Guidelines For A New Start. I pray they are a blessing to you – and that you will use and share them.

# 10 Guidelines For A New Start

1) **Be Intimate With God.** Be prayerful. Remember dependence and helplessness in your relationship with God are prerequisites for spiritual health. How about a thorough spiritual check-up this year **(2 Corinthians 13:5)**.

2) **Be Kind To Others.** Be helpful. Make a commitment to show love and encouragement to someone everyday (Romans 14:19-22). Challenge yourself to be kind and helpful especially to those who least expect it **(Ephesians 4:32)**.

3) **Cleanse Your Mind.** Read and think about something noble and creative every day **(Philippians 4:8)**. Start the day with the Bible. Let the words of life fill your heart and mind before anything else gets to them!

4) **Express Feelings With Love And Honesty Daily.** Whether fear, guilt, grief, rage, shame, or anxiety, express your feelings to God, self, and a trusted friend. **(Proverbs 27:5; 1 Pet 3:7)**

5) **Be Aware Of Your Actions.** Be generous. Without thought of reward or praise be extravagant in your giving to others **(2 Corinthians 9:7).** Give freely of your love, time, money, spirit, creativity, encouragement and praise. Don't be stingy with the most important and powerful gifts in your possession, let your actions reflect the startling love of God!

6) **Being Humble And Being Successful Work Together.** Be thankful **(Colossians 3:15).** Most, if not all of your successes are the result of God's grace, not your cleverness of hard work. Count your blessings daily.

7) **Trouble Is Temporary.** Be trustful in your faith. For seemingly mysterious reasons, many times God has chosen to make you mature through trials and hardships **(Hebrews 12:6-10).** Look for the hand of God in every circumstance and trust His guidance in the highs and lows of life.

8) **Guard Your Heart.** Be Careful **(Proverbs 23:7).** Focus your love on the Father and Savior who resides within you. Be careful what you allow to creep into this sacred space which belongs to God.

9) **Practice Daily Worship.** Be still **(Psalm 46:10).** Expressing your love and adoration to God isn't reserved for Sunday's only. Don't get too busy throughout the week to make continual

offerings of praise to God. Jesus is Lord every day!

10) **Don't Allow Sin To Enslave You.** Be repentant. Don't let any sin harden your heart or break the connection between you and God. Confess your sins to the Father every day **(I John 1:6-10)**. Claim his promises that forgive you and make you pure and clean by the blood of Jesus!

*You are highly favored, fearfully and wonderfully made!*

*Be Blessed!*

# *Acknowledgements*

I thank my Lord and Savior Jesus Christ because without Him none of this would be possible.

Thanks to my mother Carla, my father Bobby, and my spiritual parents James & Missouri Berry, for always setting a good example for me, praying for me and for sharing their wisdom about life with me. Thanks to Cynthia Turner for being a spiritual powerhouse as my prayer partner who influenced me to strive for greatness according to God's will and to never give up. Thanks to Legacy Books & Café for the opportunity to develop my career as a writer, poet and motivational speaker. Special thanks to all the St. Louis Poets who encouraged me, inspired me to write, perform, and to never give up on my dreams.

Heartfelt thanks to my best friends Joe Whitfield for always being my voice of reason and alter ego, Nurse Washington aka Robert Sr. for always keeping it brutally honest and for your sense of humor. Ruth Gholar for being supportive & my sounding board when I needed it most, Danita Smith & Latonja Flowers for having vision, a strong work ethic and for pushing me to pursue my passion as an entrepreneur. Rennell Parker for always believing in me, helping me push past my fears, providing me with the necessary resources to help me achieve my goals and for being available to brainstorm, proof read or listen to my ideas. Katraya Williams for being an example of how to follow my passion. Sharee Galvin for showing me how to never give up on my dream or vision. Selena Johnson for all of your love, encouragement, and support to be the best me through meditation.

I would like to thank Centreville, Ferguson Heights, and Southside Churches of Christ for all of your prayers and support from the beginning of my journey and for my spiritual growth along the way…and for always encouraging and volunteering me when I didn't know it. Thanks to my ministers Ralph P. Smith, Thomas Jackson, C.L. Spivey, Westley Leonard, and Conley Gibbs, Jr. for leading by example to always strive for greatness, no matter how tired, restless, or weary you may have been. You truly care about everyone you meet and have a special way of making others feel like they are the most important persons in the world.

I would like to thank my aunts, uncles, cousins, nieces, and nephews for always being true to who they are. Thanks to all of those who have played an integral part in my life during the good times, bad times and ugly times. It is because of you, and my experiences that I am able to write the pieces that you will read in this book.

# *About The Author*

—— ૐ ——

Brandy Gates was born and raised in Oakland, California, and has called Missouri her home for most of the past decade. Having two careers, Brandy has been a Law Enforcement Officer since 2009 and has served her country as a Navy Seabee Reservist since 2010, surviving an IED attack in Kabul, Afghanistan during a 2014 deployment. She has a heart for those needing to experience healing, forgiveness and understanding. Brandy writes and recites poetry to inspire, encourage and stretch people to push past comfort zones and to walk in purpose.

The middle child of eight, she is a mentor through her church and the Big Brother Big Sister program, and serves the homeless through an organization called, "Feed My Peeps." Brandy is a free spirit and is known for the unique hats she wears. Her motto is, "Changing the world one smile at a time."

Brandy Gates graduated from Louisiana Tech University and Missouri Baptist University with a Bachelor's and Master's Degree in Business

Administration respectively. She also holds a Massage Therapy Degree. A renowned poet, Brandy has performed at many venues throughout the St. Louis and Southern Illinois Metropolitan areas. She has participated for several years as a relationship panelist for The Father's Support Center which teaches males how to mend, blend and heal the relationships with the mothers of their children and relationships from their pasts.

# *About This Book*

—— ⚜ ——

Thank you for purchasing this copy of *Through My Eyes*. 15% of the proceeds from this book will be donated to Ferguson Heights Church of Christ to continue to support the ministry work which serves the people in the Ferguson community.

Brandy Gates is a poet, motivational speaker, and author.

For bookings please email the author at Brandywinedst@gmail.com.

Follow her on Instagram @Bbodacious06,

Twitter @SBE_BrandyGates

Facebook: Bethany Rucker

**May God bless you and keep you in all your endeavors.**

CPSIA information can be obtained
at www.ICGtesting.com
Printed in the USA
FFOW05n1830200117